A

GARDEN

Of

THOUGHTS

MY AFFIRMATION
J O U R N A L

A Writing Companion
For A Journey Into Self-Discovery

Louise L. Hay

HAY HOUSE, INC.
Santa Monica, CA

A GARDEN OF THOUGHTS
My Affirmation Journal
Copyright © 1989 by Louise L. Hay

Hay House, Inc.
Santa Monica, California

Art direction: Gwen Rainey-Smith
Cover design: Kevin Pike and Gwen Rainey-Smith
Editors: Andrew Ettinger, Dan Olmos, and Valerie A. Marz
Typesetting: Eurotype, Inc., Santa Monica, CA
Printing: Delta Lithograph Co., Valencia, CA
Based on a concept by Barton Jay

Printed in the United States of America

Library of Congress categories: New Age/Inspirational/Self-Help

First Printing September 1989

ISBN 0-937611-67-0

10 9 8 7 6 5 4 3 2

DEDICATED TO YOU

Please join me in filling this journal with treasured thoughts and new ideas. Together we can help create a loving world.

The Power of
Your Own Inner Expression

This journal was designed to inspire you, to help you explore your own power of self-expression, and to provide a creative forum for your thoughts. Louise's affirmations may be used as a guiding light, to spark your own thoughts, feelings, and personal affirmations.

Like any tool used for self-discovery, growth, and healing, journal writing takes practice. Patience and consistency are the underlying requisites for change and growth.

"Journal-keeping is a means of documenting the spontaneous flow of your life and growth. It is a vehicle for experiencing the present more fully and also witnessing past patterns and setting goals for the future," writes Lucia Capacchione in her classic work, *The Creative Journal*.

Journal writing is a practice you can integrate into your lifestyle as you move forward on your path of self-discovery. Make a quiet time and space for yourself in which to write. No need to be rigid about this, because then writing may become something to dread — like a chore or a homework assignment. Let the time you set aside for yourself to write be a time of quiet meditation and introspection.

It may also be worthwhile for you to keep your journal with you during the day so that you can take advantage of spare moments to record observations, describe new ideas, or to capture those sudden flashes of personal insight.

You can write about your experiences and feelings, what you are going through, and how you feel about it. You may choose to express yourself through drawings, symbols, or scribbles.

If you wish, let your inner child come out and play. Try different writing tools: colored pens or pencils, crayons, or ink pens. Be spontaneous — have fun — don't worry about spelling, grammar, or neatness. It is your personal journal — and your *journey* — so express yourself in whatever way you feel most comfortable. The results may surprise you.

In the private space of your journal, you will discover the clarity of your inner voice. Journal writing allows you a special view of your inner self.

If you choose to share your journal, take care to choose only people with whom you share absolute trust and love. Put your inner-critic aside. If what you discover is negative, don't be frightened. Acknowledge that part of yourself — know that everyone has negativity to overcome — and then use it as an opportunity to create positive new thoughts and images to replace the old.

We trust that this journal will be a safe and inspiring place for you to record your thoughts, feelings, and affirmations, a place to give shape to your hopes and dreams . . . it may be a portrait of a new and enlightening time in your life.

— the editors

The Power of Affirmations
By Louise L. Hay

Affirmations are really anything we say or think. Our thoughts create our feelings, beliefs, and experiences. Too often they are negative. We say "I don't want this in my life" or "I don't want to be sick anymore" or "I hate this job." If we want to change or manifest something in our lives, we must state what we *do* want. We must *affirm* that we are willing to see ourselves or our lives in a different perspective. Thus, we can change our experiences by first changing our thoughts.

When you first start using an affirmation it may not seem true for you. If it were already true, you would not need the affirmation.

Think of what happens when you plant a seed. First it germinates, then it sprouts roots, and then it pokes its first shoot up through the ground. It takes time to go from a seed to a full grown plant. And so it is with affirmations. Be gentle and patient with yourself.

You may also experience some doubt as to whether you are doing the affirmations correctly or even whether the affirmations are doing you any good at all. This is perfectly normal.

You see, the subconscious mind is like a filing cabinet — all the thoughts, words, and experiences you have had since birth get filed away, like messages. Think of your mind as having a team of couriers who grab the messages, look at them, and put them in the appropriate files. Perhaps you have been building up files for years, with messages like "I'm not good enough," "I'm not smart enough to do that," or "Why bother?" The subconscious gets absolutely buried under these files.

Suddenly, when the couriers begin seeing messages that say, "I'm wonderful and I love myself," they respond with, "What is this? Where do we file this? We've never seen this message before."

That's when they call in Doubt. Doubt picks up the message and says to you, "Hey, look at this. We have no place to file this one — it must be a mistake." You can either say to Doubt, "Oh, you're right. I'm terrible. I'm not good. Sorry, I made a mistake," and go back to your old way of thinking. Or, you can say to Doubt, "Thank you for sharing, but this is the *new* message. Set up a new file because there are going to be lots of these coming through." By doing this, over time, you will change your thinking and create a new reality for yourself. Remember, *you* are in charge.

Reinforce your new positive affirmations in any way you can: in your thoughts, your conversations with yourself and others, and by writing them down in this journal. We created this journal to inspire you on your path to personal growth and healing. You may choose to use the affirmations on each page as a springboard to creating your own. Once you find affirmations that are right for you, you may want to put them up on your mirror, on your desk, or on your car dashboard.

Remember, one thought does not mean much. But thoughts that we think over and over are like drops of water: at first there are just a few; and then after awhile you've created a pool, and then a lake, and then an ocean. If our thinking is negative, we can drown in a sea of negativity; if it's positive, we can float on the ocean of life.

I open myself to new ideas and new horizons.

I trust my Higher Self. I listen with love to my inner voice. I release all that is unlike the action of love.

*I am one with the Power that created me and this Power
has given me the power to create my own circumstances.
I rejoice in the knowledge that I have the power of
my own mind to use in any way I choose.*

I am willing to release old negative beliefs.
They are only thoughts that stand in my way.
My new thoughts are positive and fulfilling.

I allow the love from my own heart to wash through me and cleanse and heal every part of my body and my emotions.

My good now flows freely.
Divine ideas express themselves through me.
I am at peace.

I radiate joy and share it with others.
It is a time for laughter and singing and dancing.
I bless everyone and everything.

It's only a thought and a thought can be changed.

Life created me to be fulfilled.
I trust life and life is always there at every turn. I am safe.

*There is no competition and no comparison
for we are all different and meant to be that way.
I am special and wonderful. I love myself.*

It is my birthright to love fully and freely.
I give to life exactly what I want life to give me.
I am glad to be alive. I love life!

I am guided throughout this day in making right choices.
Divine Intelligence continuously guides me
in the realization of my goals. I am safe.

I turn every experience into an opportunity.

*Whatever I am guided to do will be a success.
I learn from every experience. My pathway is a series of
stepping stones to ever greater successes.
Today is my stepping stone to new awareness and greater glory.*

I flow freely and lovingly with life. I love myself.
I know only good awaits me at every turn.

I rejoice in other's successes, knowing there is plenty for all.
I am constantly increasing my conscious awareness of abundance,
and this reflects in a constantly increasing income.

My good comes from everywhere and everyone.

I am in the perfect place and I am safe at all times.

The Ocean of Life is lavish with its abundance.
All my needs and desires are met before I even ask.
My good comes from everywhere and everyone and everything.

I claim my own power and I lovingly create my own reality.

Love is everywhere, and I am lovable.
Loving people fill my life,
and I find myself easily expressing love to others.

I am powerful and capable. I love and appreciate all of myself.

I am open and receptive to strength, happiness, and peace.
I choose to build my life upon hope, courage, and love.

I now accept all good as normal and natural for me.
Love is a miraculous healing power in my world.
Using love, I am in charge of rebuilding my life.

I trust my inner voice. I am strong, wise, and powerful.

We all have tremendous wisdom within us. Inside of us all are the answers to all the questions we shall ever ask.

Forgiveness is the answer to almost every problem.
Forgiveness is a gift to myself.
I forgive and I set myself free.

Deep in the center of my being, there is an infinite well of love.
I now allow this love to flow to the surface. It fills my heart,
my body, my mind, my consciousness, my very being,
and radiates out from me in all directions
and returns to me multiplied.

I open my consciousness to the expansion of life.

My mind is gentle and harmonious.
I love and approve of myself.
I am free to be me.

I accept all this abundant life with joy and pleasure and gratitude. I am deserving.

I only give out that which I wish to receive in return.
My love and acceptance of others is mirrored to me in every moment.

Peace of mind is mine.

I lovingly release others to their own lessons.
I lovingly care for myself. I move with ease through life.

Divine peace and harmony surround me and dwell in me.
I feel tolerance, compassion, and love for all people.

There is a rhythm and flow to life and I am part of it.
Life supports me and brings to me only good and positive experiences.
I trust the process of life to bring me my highest good.

I accept my power, and I now allow my own uniqueness to express itself in deeply fulfilling ways.

*My unique creative talents and abilities flow through me
and are expressed in deeply satisfying ways.
My creativity is always in demand.*

I am completely supported by the Universe. I trust life to unfold before me in positive ways. I now discover how wonderful I am. I choose to love and enjoy myself.

I am lovable and I am loved. I am worth loving.

I am free to think wonderful thoughts.
I move beyond past limitations into freedom.
I am now becoming all that I was created to be.

This is a new day. One that I have never lived before.
I stay in the Now and enjoy each and every moment.

I celebrate today, another precious day on earth.
I shall live it with joy. Today I am a new person.

I relax and free my thoughts. I am at peace.
I am a free person living in a world that is a reflection
of my own love and understanding.

I marvel at the miracle that is my body. I choose the healing thoughts that create and maintain my healthy body and make me feel good.

Now is a time for healing, for making whole.
We must rise out of the limitations of the past.
We are all divine, magnificent expressions of life.

I know I am worthwhile. It is safe for me to succeed. Life loves me.

I am part of the symphony of life. I unite myself with harmony; my mind is centered on peace. I am in harmony with all of life.

I look in the mirror and say "I love you, I really love you."
As I continue to do this simple affirmation,
my inner energy begins to shift.
I am now able to see my own beauty and magnificence.

I sleep peacefully. I trust the process of life to be on my side and take care of everything for my highest good and greatest joy.

It is my mind that creates my experiences.
I am unlimited in my own ability to create the good in my life.

The past has no power over me because I am willing to learn
and to change. I see my past as necessary
to bring me where I am today.
I am willing to begin where I am right now.

Every thought I think is creating my future.

It is with flexibility and ease that I see all sides of an issue.
There are endless ways of doing things and seeing things.
I am safe.

In the infinity of life where I am, all is perfect, whole and complete, and yet life is ever-changing.

*There is no beginning and no end,
only a constant cycling and recycling
of substance and experiences. Life is never static or stale,
for each moment is ever new and fresh.*

All that I need to know at any given moment is revealed to me.
I trust myself and I trust life. All is well.

I open my heart and exchange the most healing gift of all —
the precious gift of unconditional love.

I move beyond old limitations and now allow myself to express myself freely and creatively.

I center myself in safety and accept the perfection of my life.
All is well.

Every experience is perfect for our growth process.
I am at peace with where I am.

The totality of possibilities lies before me.
I deserve a good life. I deserve good health.
I deserve joy and happiness.
I deserve freedom, freedom to be all that I can be.

In my mind, I have total freedom. I now move into a new space in consciousness where I am willing to see myself differently. I am willing to create new thoughts about myself and about my life.

I declare peace and harmony within me and around me.

I am willing to learn whatever I need to learn.
I am willing to change and to grow. I now attract to myself
everything I need on the physical level to help me.

I give myself permission to be all that I can be.
I deserve the very best in life.
I love and appreciate myself and others.

We are all doing the best we can at any point in time and space.
We make our positive changes much quicker and easier
when we love each other unconditionally.

I can look into my eyes and say: "I forgive you and I love you."
As I forgive myself, I can more easily forgive others.

I deserve all good.

I relax into the flow of life and let life provide all that I need easily and comfortably. Life is for me.

I open myself to the wisdom within,
knowing that there is only One Intelligence in this Universe.
Out of this One Intelligence comes all the answers,
all the solutions, all the healing, all the creation.

*I trust this Power and Intelligence,
knowing that whatever I need to know
is revealed to me in the right time, space, and sequence.
All is well in my world.*

I am completely open to life and joy.
I choose to see with love.

I now go beyond other people's fears and limitations.
I create my life.

The spiritual food required by my mind and body is a constant flow of love. I show love to myself in a panorama of ways.

I see this love expressed
in the choices I make for myself.
I feel it in the love I surround myself with.

I lovingly balance my mind and my body.
I now choose thoughts that make me feel good.

Each moment of my life is new and fresh and vital.
I use my affirmative thinking to create exactly what I want.

*Harmony surrounds me. I listen with love
to the pleasant and the good. I am a center for love.*

*I am a powerful being. I am the only thinker in my mind.
No matter what others tell me, I make the decision
to accept or reject it. My power lies in my thoughts.*

I am open to the new and changing.
Every moment presents a wonderful new opportunity
to become more of who I am.

I flow with life easily and effortlessly.

I am filled with life and energy and the joy of living.

I bless my body. I am grateful for my body. I love my body.

My body becomes more precious to me with each passing day.
I love this temple, the classroom that I live within.

*I create peacefulness in my mind
and my body reflects this peacefulness as perfect health.*

I have the power and the strength and knowledge to handle everything in my life.

I do not need to struggle for change.
The change that is for my good happens automatically
as I allow it. I release with ease.

I radiate acceptance and I am deeply loved by others.
Love surrounds me and protects me.

I now receive my good from expected and unexpected sources.
I am an unlimited being, accepting from an unlimited source,
in an unlimited way. I am blessed beyond my fondest dreams.

I am enthusiastic about life and filled with energy.

I move forward in life with joy and with ease.

I think and speak only words of love.
I am at peace with life.
I speak with gentleness and love.

*Life mirrors my every thought. As I keep my thoughts positive,
Life brings to me only good experiences.*

I love myself, therefore I provide myself with a comfortable home,
one that fills all my needs and is a pleasure to be in.
I fill the rooms with the vibration of love so that all who enter
will feel this love and be nourished by it.

My mental atmosphere of love and acceptance is a magnet
for small miracles every moment of the day.
Where I am, there is a healing atmosphere,
and it blesses and brings peace to all.

I love myself. I behave and think in a loving way to all people for I know that what I give out returns to me multiplied.

There is time and space for everything I want to do.

*I see the best in everyone and help them
to bring out their most joyous qualities.*

I lovingly release the day and slip into peaceful sleep,
knowing tomorrow will take care of itself.

Every moment of life is a new beginning point as we move from the old. This moment is a new point of beginning for me right here and right now.

I am at peace just where I am. I accept my good, knowing all my needs and desires will be fulfilled.

I easily flow with change. My life is Divinely guided and I am always going in the best direction.

Every thought I think creates my future.
I release all false ideas and dis-ease with every exhalation.
I affirm love for myself and for life with every inhalation.

Within each of us there is a special place where we are connected with the entire Universe. We bring our awareness to this place and we are conscious of the connection of body, mind, and emotion.

I am grounded in my own power.

By choosing loving, joyous thoughts,
I create a loving, joyous world. I am safe and free.

As I rejoice in new growth, change and surprise are evident.
Life awakens and beauty is everywhere.
I look with delight at all I see.

I am on an endless journey through eternity
and there is plenty of time.
I communicate with love.

I recognize my own intuitive ability.

I approve of myself, and my decisions are always perfect for me.

I trust my inner voice. I am strong, wise, and powerful.

I am grateful for life's generosity to me. I am blessed.

With my loving attitude I help create a world where it is safe for us to love each other.

I release all that is unlike love and joy in my mind.
I move from the past into the new and fresh and vital.

There is plenty of space for me to grow and to change.

I handle all my experiences with wisdom,
with love, and with ease.

I envision a world of peace and plenty.
I feel harmony and unity between nations,
and I contribute to that harmony.

Every ending is a new beginning. Life is eternal.

About the Author

Louise L. Hay, author of the international bestseller *You Can Heal Your Life*, is a metaphysical teacher and lecturer. Her concepts of "loving the self" form the foundation for her techniques and philosophy. Through her teachings many people have learned how to create more of what they want in their lives, including greater wellness in their bodies, minds, and spirits.

According to Ms. Hay, "There is no new knowledge. All is ancient and infinite. It is my joy and pleasure to gather together wisdom and knowledge for the benefit of those on the healing pathway."

"I don't heal anyone. The work I do is to help people to understand how their own mental patterns are constantly creating their own life experiences . . . and also, how these same mental patterns are contributing to the ease and dis-ease in their bodies," Ms. Hay says.

Ms. Hay is a Church of Religious Science minister and holds a Doctor of Divinity degree from the Science of Mind College. She has also studied in a wide range of New Thought schools and continues to participate as an inspirational leader in promoting principles of positive thinking and healing.

As founder of Hay House, Inc., and the Hay Institute, Ms. Hay makes frequent media appearances, sponsors major workshops and symposiums, and publishes books, audio tapes, and video cassettes that focus on information that provides guidance and insight into how love and understanding can heal people and, indeed, our planet.

Lousie L. Hay currently lives in Southern California, not far from her publishing and institute headquarters in Santa Monica.

If you would like to receive a catalog of Hay House products or information about future workshops, lectures and events sponsored by the Louise L. Hay Educational Institute, please detach and mail the questionnaire below.

To: HAY HOUSE, INC.
P. O. Box 2212
Santa Monica, CA 90406

To: HAY HOUSE, INC.
P. O. Box 2212
Santa Monica, CA 90406

We hope you receive value from *A Garden Of Thoughts*. Please help us to evaluate our distribution program by filling out the brief questionnaire below. Upon receipt of this postcard, your catalog will be sent promptly.

NAME _____

ADDRESS _____

_____

I purchased this book from

☐ Store _____

   City _____

☐ Other (Catalog, Lecture, Workshop)

   Specify _____

Occupation _____ Age _____

We hope you receive value from *A Garden Of Thoughts*. Please help us to evaluate our distribution program by filling out the brief questionnaire below. Upon receipt of this postcard, your catalog will be sent promptly.

NAME _____

ADDRESS _____

_____

I purchased this book from

☐ Store _____

   City _____

☐ Other (Catalog, Lecture, Workshop)

   Specify _____

Occupation _____ Age _____